World Book, Inc.
180 North LaSalle Street
Suite 900
Chicago, Illinois 60601
USA

For information about other "True or False?" titles, as
well as other World Book print and digital publications,
please go to www.worldbook.com.

For information about other World Book publications,
call 1-800-WORLDBK (967-5325).

For information about sales to schools and libraries,
call 1-800-975-3250 (United States) or 1-800-837-5365
(Canada).

Library of Congress Cataloging-in-Publication Data for
this volume has been applied for.

True or False?
ISBN: 978-0-7166-3761-5 (set, hc.)

Outlaws
ISBN: 978-0-7166-3766-0 (hc.)

Also available as:
ISBN: 978-0-7166-3776-9 (e-book, ePUB3)

Printed in China by RR Donnelley,
Guangdong Province
1st printing May 2019

Staff

Executive Committee

President
Geoff Broderick

Vice President, Finance
Donald D. Keller

Vice President, Marketing
Jean Lin

Vice President, International
Maksim Rutenberg

Vice President, Technology
Jason Dole

Director, Human Resources
Bev Ecker

Editorial

Director, New Print
Tom Evans

Writer
Mellonee Carrigan

Editor
Shawn Brennan

Librarian
S. Thomas Richardson

Manager, Contracts and
Compliance
(Rights and Permissions)
Loranne K. Shields

Manager, Indexing Services
David Pofelski

Digital

Director, Digital Product
Development
Erika Meller

Digital Product Manager
Jonathan Wills

Graphics and Design

Senior Art Director
Tom Evans

Senior Visual
Communications Designer
Melanie Bender

Media Editor
Rosalia Bledsoe

Manufacturing/Production

Manufacturing Manager
Anne Fritzinger

Production Specialist
Curley Hunter

Proofreader
Nathalie Strassheim

OUTLAWS

WORLD
BOOK

www.worldbook.com

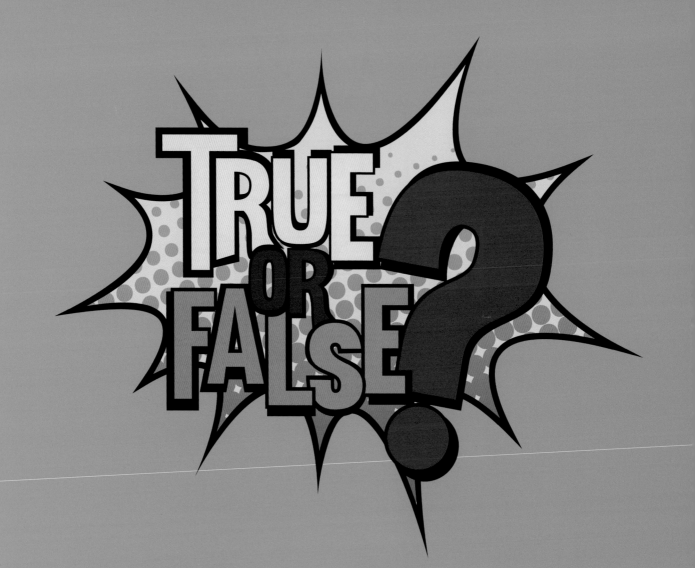

Outlaws only existed in the Wild West.

4

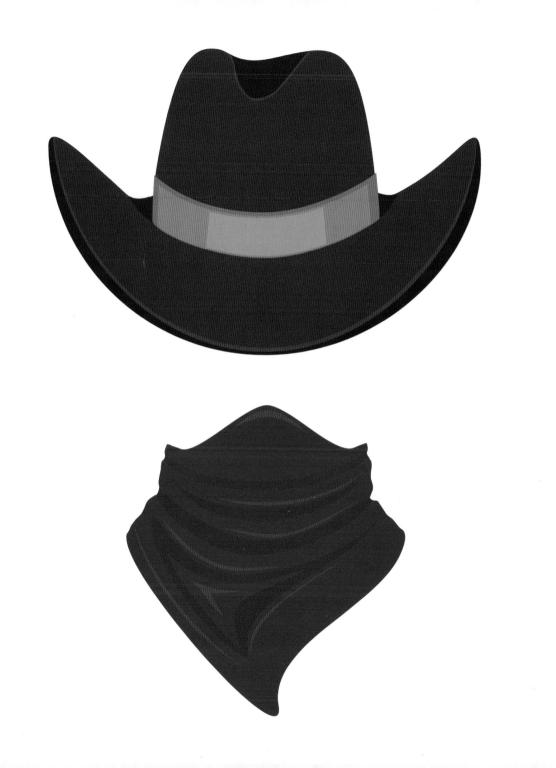

5

An outlaw is any criminal. But when we think of outlaws, we often think of bandits, robbers, and gunfighters from the American frontier period nicknamed the "Wild West" or "Old West." This book will talk about some of the most infamous outlaws from the Wild West, as well as some notorious outlaws from other time periods!

The notorious Jesse James was a preacher's son.

TRUE!

Jesse James's father, Robert, was a Baptist minister and farmer. When Jesse was a small boy, his father went to California to preach to the gold miners.

Jesse James (1847-1882) was one of the most famous bank and train robbers in the history of the United States. He led about 25 robberies in Missouri and several other states. His gang also killed a number of people.

The gangster couple Bonnie and Clyde stole lots of cash during their bank robberies.

Bonnie and Clyde were American outlaws who engaged in a spree of murders and robberies during the early 1930's. Their crime spree swept across rural towns in the Midwest and Southwest United States.

The amounts Bonnie and Clyde managed to steal were usually less than $100 and sometimes as little as $5 or $10.

**A lady dressed in red helped catch
the notorious criminal John Dillinger.**

TRUE!

Dillinger was hiding in Chicago when his friend Anna Sage betrayed him on July 22, 1934. Sage told federal agents she would be wearing a red dress when she went with Dillinger to the Biograph theater that night to see a movie. Federal agents fatally shot Dillinger as he left the theater. Sage became famous as the "woman in red."

TRUE OR FALSE?

The legendary outlaw Butch Cassidy was named after his father.

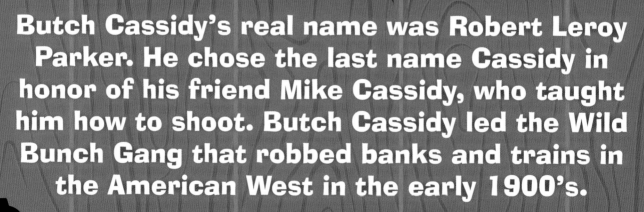

FALSE!

Butch Cassidy's real name was Robert Leroy Parker. He chose the last name Cassidy in honor of his friend Mike Cassidy, who taught him how to shoot. Butch Cassidy led the Wild Bunch Gang that robbed banks and trains in the American West in the early 1900's.

$4,000 Reward

WILL BE PAID FOR THE CAPTURE OF ROBERT LEROY PARKER

DEAD OR ALIVE

Age, 36 years (1901)
Weight, 165 lbs.
Complexion, Light.
Eyes, Blue.
Nationality, American.
Marks, two cut scars back of head, small scar under left eye, small brown mole calf of leg.

Height, 5 ft. 9 in.
Build, Medium.
Color of hair, Flaxen.
Mustache, sandy if any
Occupation, Cowboy, Rustler.
Criminal occupation, bank robber & Highwaym cattle and horse thief.

ROBERT LEROY PARKER

ALIAS

"BUTCH" CASSIDY

23

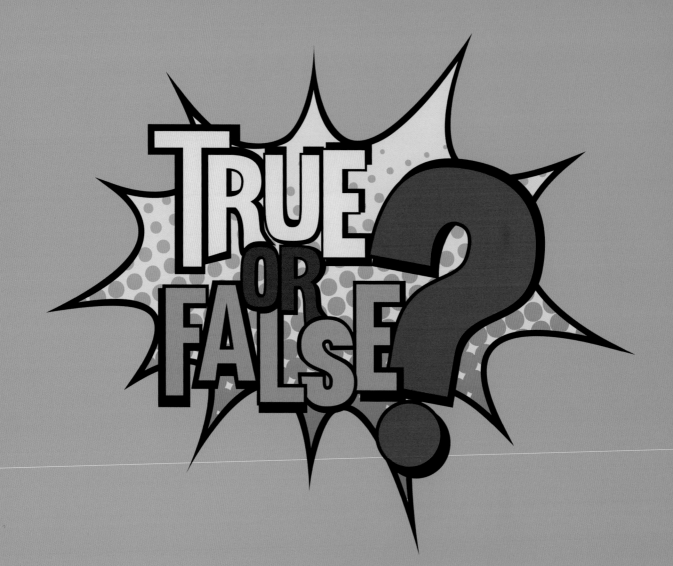

The gunfighter called the Sundance Kid was from Sundance, Wyoming.

Harry Alonzo Longabaugh, better known as the Sundance Kid, was born in Mont Clare, Pennsylvania. He got his nickname from stealing horses in Sundance, Wyoming. Sundance and fellow outlaw Butch Cassidy led the Wild Bunch Gang in robbing banks and trains in the early 1900's. Sundance was said to be the fastest gunfighter of the bunch.

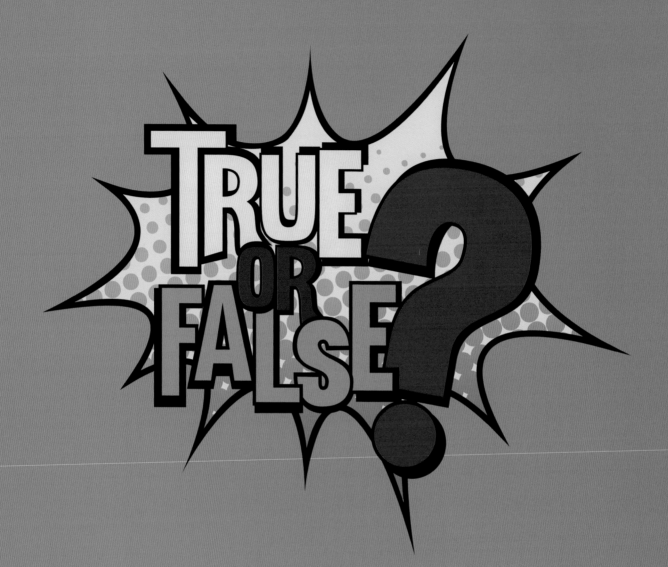

Belle Starr, one of the few female outlaws in the United States, was known as the Bandit Queen.

Belle Starr's cabin became a hideout for other bandits, including Jesse James and his brother Frank. Starr was a robber and cattle and horse thief in the Southwest in the mid-1800's.

TRUE OR FALSE?

Belle Starr's real name was
Annie Oakley.

Starr's real name was Myra Maybelle
Shirley. She called herself Belle and
became known as Belle Starr after her
marriage to a Cherokee named Sam Starr.

Annie Oakley was not an outlaw.
She was a famous American
sharpshooter in the late 1800's.

Lawmen used photographs to prove an outlaw's death.

Photographs also confirmed the deaths of outlaws for rewards that may have been offered on "WANTED" posters for outlaws, captured "dead or alive."

The famous outlaw Billy the Kid never robbed a bank or train.

Billy the Kid was a *rustler* (cattle thief) and killer in New Mexico in the late 1870's. He stole cattle and a horse or two. But he never held up a bank, train, or stagecoach. The Kid also killed at least five men—some legends say he killed as many as 21. Billy the Kid's real name was Henry McCarty. But he often used his stepfather's name, William.

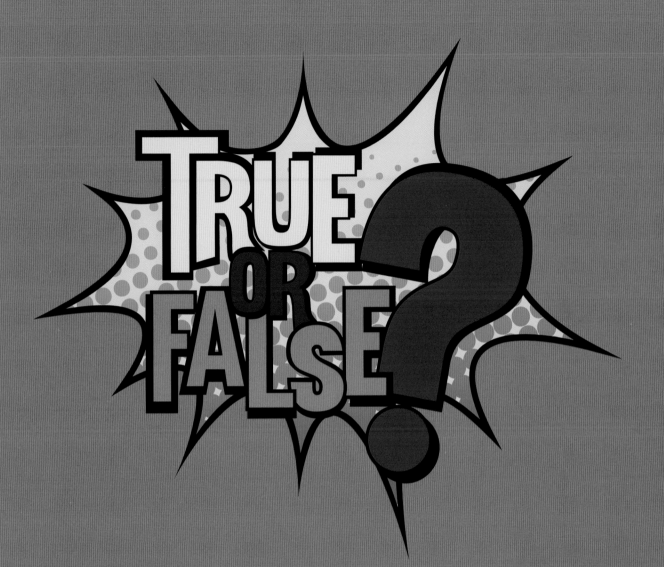

**Billy the Kid's favorite hat
was a top hat.**

The Kid often wore a tall
Mexican sombrero with a
wide decorative band.

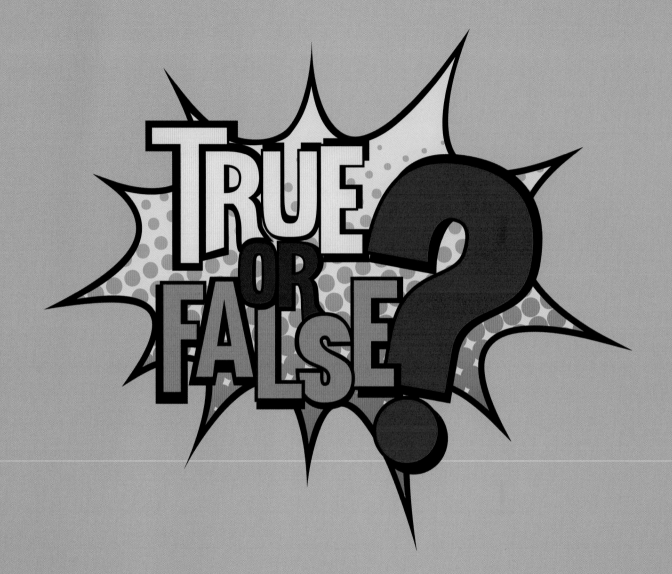

The gunfighter Doc Holliday was a dentist.

TRUE!

John Henry "Doc" Holliday graduated near the top of his class in 1872 at what was then the Pennsylvania College of Dental Surgery. He worked as a dentist for a time before becoming a gambler and gunfighter. In 1881, Doc Holliday was involved in the famous shootout at the O.K. Corral in Tombstone, Arizona.

Holliday joined his friend Wyatt Earp and Earp's two brothers, who represented the law, in the Tombstone gunfight against a gang of cowboys and cattle rustlers known as the Clantons and the McLaurys. Three of the cowboys were killed, and three of the lawmen were wounded, including Doc Holliday.

The FBI is still searching for the modern-day outlaw D. B. Cooper, more than 40 years after he jumped out of an airplane with a bag of money and disappeared.

53

The FBI ended its long search in 2016 for the infamous hijacker who called himself Dan Cooper. A journalist wrote down D. B. Cooper by mistake, but the name stuck. In 1971, Cooper *hijacked* (took over by force) an airplane and jumped out of it over the Pacific Northwest. He was carrying $200,000 in ransom money. Some of the money was found in 1980. But Cooper was never seen again.

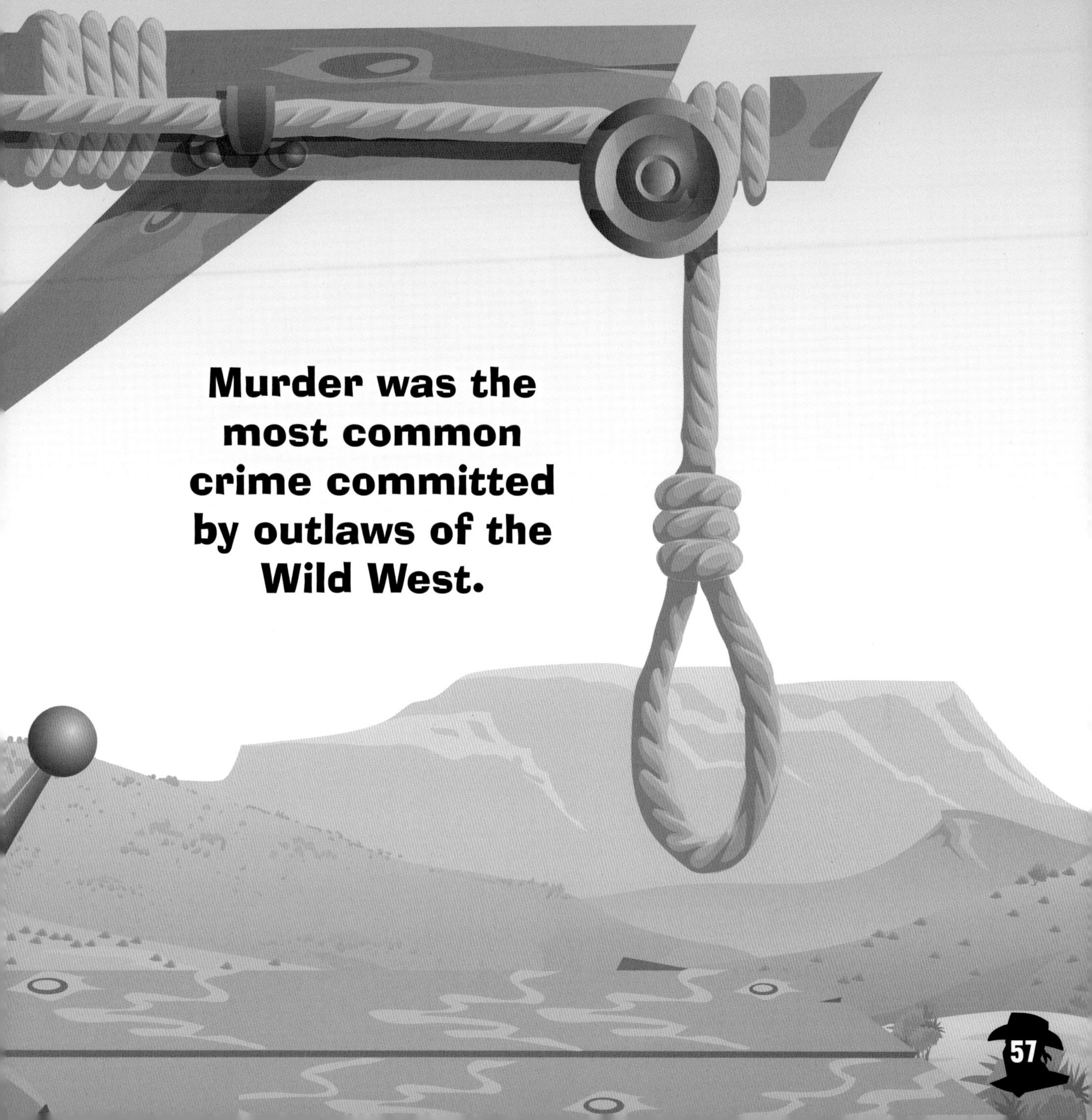

Murder was the
most common
crime committed
by outlaws of the
Wild West.

Outlaws committed more bank and train robberies than any other crime during the Wild West days of the mid- to late 1800's.

TRUE OR FALSE?

Texas outlaw Sam Bass was known
as "the baddest man in the West."

FALSE!

Bass was known as a "good badman." He was a good-hearted outlaw in the 1870's who led a band of bank and train robbers in Texas. According to legend, he shared what he stole with the poor. His legend has been kept alive by stories of his generosity and by the ballad that bears his name, "The Ballad of Sam Bass."

TRUE OR FALSE?

Jesse James tried to stay out of the spotlight. That way, he'd never get caught!

Jesse James loved getting public attention. The outlaw wrote letters to newspapers defending his actions. He even handed out press releases at the scene of his robberies!

Breaking News

The outlaw nicknamed "Black Jack" Ketchum was notorious for stealing money while gambling.

Black Jack, whose real name was Thomas Edward Ketchum, was the leader of the Ketchum Gang of train robbers.

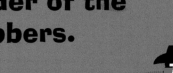

TRUE OR FALSE?

Cherokee Bill was a ruthless black Indian outlaw.

Crawford Goldsby, better known as Cherokee Bill, had mixed-race parents. His father claimed to be of black, Sioux, Mexican, and white ancestry. His mother was said to be a mixed black and Cherokee woman. Cherokee Bill ran with a group of other black Indian outlaws who committed a series of violent crimes across Indian Territory (now Oklahoma) in the mid-1890's.

Cherokee Bill got his name from his Cherokee heritage and the town of Cherokee, Kansas, where he attended an Indian school. In Cherokee country, the name "Bill" meant "wild hand"—a person not to be disagreed with.

Infamous gangster Al Capone had the nickname Snorky.

Snorky is a slang term meaning spiffy or smartly dressed. Al Capone's friends called him Snorky. However, Capone was better known by another nickname— Scarface. He was called Scarface because his left cheek was slashed in a fight.

Robin Hood was a real person.

81

Many scholars believe that Robin Hood is a fictitious character. However, according to one scholar, Robin Hood was actually the Earl of Huntingdon, and his real name was Robert Fitzooth. Robin Hood was an English outlaw who stole from the rich and gave to the poor.

TRUE OR FALSE?

Doc Holliday's girlfriend Big Mouth Kate got her name because she snitched on the gang.

FALSE!

Holliday's girlfriend was known as Big Nose Kate because of her prominent nose. Her real name was Mary Katharine Haroney. She once helped Holliday escape from jail by setting it on fire.

TRUE OR FALSE?

Ned Kelly was Australia's most famous *bushranger* (outlaw). Bushrangers were criminals who operated in rural Australia from about 1790 to 1900.

TRUE!

Kelly has become a legendary folk hero in Australia. Through the years, some people have considered him to be a cruel and vicious criminal. Others have admired him as a symbol of revolt against authority and injustice. The bushrangers' crimes usually involved cattle theft, highway robbery, and murder. During the early years, their crimes also included *cannibalism* (eating people).

DID YOU KNOW...

WANTED

Four Texas brothers known as the Newton Gang committed more bank and train robberies than all those by the Dalton Gang and gangs led by Jesse James and Butch Cassidy combined. Willis, Doc, Joe, and Hess Newton claimed they pulled off **nearly 100 heists in the 1920's.**

Henry Newton Brown was both an outlaw and a lawman in 1880's Kansas. He rode with Billy the Kid's gang before becoming marshal of Caldwell, Kansas. Brown won praise for cleaning up the town, but soon returned to his criminal ways. He was caught after trying to rob a bank.

The Mexican brothers Felipe and Jose Espanosas

led a gang of cousins who terrorized white settlers in the Colorado Territory in 1863.

The Bandit Queen, born Myra Maybelle Shirley, lived the life of a **spoiled, rich girl** before turning to a life of crime.

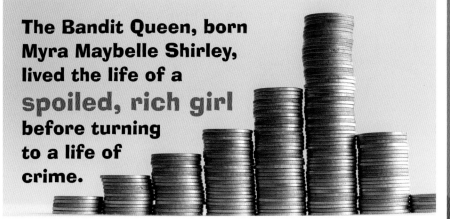

The Apache Kid was an Indian scout for the U.S. Army before he became an outlaw in New Mexico

and Arizona territories in the late 1800's.

Hoodoo Brown was the baddest outlaw around in 1879. He led the Dodge City Gang while serving as mayor of Las Vegas, New Mexico. Brown's real name was Hyman G. Neill. **Brown used his position** to cover up crimes committed by him and his gang of murderous gunfighters and gamblers.

Index

Acknowledgments

Cover: © Elnur/Shutterstock; © Rufat Alisultanli, Shutterstock
5-25   © Shutterstock
26   Public Domain
29   © Shutterstock
30   Public Domain
33   Library of Congress
35   Public Domain
37-39   © Shutterstock
40   © Shutterstock; Public Domain
42-46   © Shutterstock
49   © dieKleinert/Alamy Images
50-60   © Shutterstock
61   © Shutterstock; Public Domain
62-73   © Shutterstock
75   Public Domain
76   Federal Bureau of Investigation
79   © Hulton Archive/Getty Images
81-84   © Shutterstock
86   © Shutterstock; Public Domain
88   © Shutterstock; State Library Victoria
89-96   © Shutterstock